Beneath

The Surface

Virginia Monroe

ISBN: -13: 979-8-218-15217-8

Table of Contents

"He that is without sin among you, let him first cast a stone at her."

John 8:7

Ch.1

La Crosse

In the beautiful state of Wisconsin, there is a place called Plainfield. This small midwestern village has undeniable charm and beauty. Yet, it will be forever haunted by a memory that most of the residents wish that they could forget. In 1957, the people of Plainfield were horrified when they realized what had taken place in their community. They lived amongst a man they thought they knew and trusted, only to find out that beneath the surface of this man, was a monster that would instill fear in the residents of Plainfield and in people around the world. This story begins one hundred and nine miles west of Plainfield, in La Crosse Wisconsin.

La Crosse is the birthplace of Edward Gein. Eddie is known as America's most notorious psychopath. He may seem like a monster but when you analyze his life you will find that he never had a chance to develop into a healthy adult. His parents had issues that were never dealt with, and those issues affected Eddie greatly. It all starts with Eddie's father George.

George was born in Vernon County, Wisconsin, on August 4th, 1873. George's parents and sister left for town on their wagon. While they were on their way, their wagon got caught in a flash flood. Sadly, they perished in the Mississippi river. All alone as a little toddler, George had to be raised by his strict and stern Scottish grandparents. He did not receive the tender affection that he needed. When he was old enough to work, he became a black smith. George had low self-esteem, and he felt lost. On the outside, he seemed calm and respectable. On the inside he dealt with emotional turmoil, and he began to drown those feelings with alcohol. Drinking was a temporary relief that ended up crippling his life. He started working in the nearby town of La Crosse. However, he could not maintain a stable situation and found himself in and out of jobs. He sold insurance, worked for a railway, the city power company, and he became skilled in tannery and carpentry. Though he acquired many skills, he felt that it all amounted to nothing.

Virginia Monroe
BENEATH THE SURFACE

One day he met Augusta Wilhelmine Lehrke. She came from a large family of German descent. Augusta was born in La Crosse on July 21, 1878. Her parents were Fred and Amalia Lerhke. They were devout Lutherans. Augusta had many siblings and lived at home until she graduated. She began working until she had to return home to care for her sick mother. August was unmarried, unlike her other sisters. In result, she was able to take care of her parents. After her mother's death, she cared for her father and younger siblings until she met George Gein. George tried his best to hide his problems from Augusta. She was very strong-willed and confident, which was quite the opposite of George. However, the unlikely pair married on December 4, 1899. George was twenty-four and Augusta was nineteen.

Because George depended heavily on alcohol, this caused Augusta to grow feelings of disdain for George. She felt betrayed that he had hidden this from her. She viewed him as a deceitful man, and she tried her best to forgive him. George admired Augusta's confidence and stability. He also admired the fact that she had a large family, since he lost his at such a young age. George knew he did not receive the same admiration from Augusta. He felt like he would never be able to live up to what she wanted him to be. Due to George's drinking, their marriage became terribly difficult but Augusta, being very religious, would not waver when it came to her beliefs. She did not belief in divorce and was willing to try everything in her power to make the marriage work.

Augusta longed for a child hoping it would fill the void in her heart. So, George and Augusta had a son on January 17, 1902. They named him Henry George Gein. During this time, Augusta felt that her struggling husband should work for himself. They decided to open a meat and grocery shop in downtown La Crosse. George could not handle the responsibility of managing the shop. In result, Augusta decided to take over the business and George was demoted to clerk. Augusta always wanted to have a girl. So, she became pregnant again and gave birth to another son on August 27, 1906. They named him Edward Theodore Gein. Disappointed that she did not conceive a girl, Augusta was determined to make sure that her sons would not grow up to become worldly men. Therefore, she felt that they needed to pursue a new life elsewhere. She also believed that La Crosse was a sinful place and did not want her boys exposed to wicked things as they grew older. She wanted to shut out the world's problems by moving to a farm far away from everything. Her desire was to isolate herself and her family, and she also hoped that George would overcome his alcohol addiction.

Ch.2

Plainfield

The Gein family packed up and moved to a farm near Camp Douglas. Their new home was secluded and unfortunately there was nowhere for Henry and Eddie to attend school. Seeing that this was a problem, they decided to move again and headed east to Plainfield. Plainfield is located on the windswept flat lands of central Wisconsin. It has always been a small, hardworking town. In 1848, a man named William N. Kelly a pioneer from New York, was the first to settle in Plainfield. At the time, he called it Norwich. One year later, Elijah C Waterman arrived from Vermont. He had a vision and laid out his plan to start a Village. He built mills to attract new settlers and offered them free lots. He became the first postmaster and changed the name from Norwich to Plainfield in Honor of his hometown Plainfield, Vermont.

By the time the Gein family arrived around 1914, Plainfield was a well-established town. Augusta felt that it would be the perfect area to start a new life. The Gein family bought a one hundred- and ninety-five-acre dairy farm six miles from the village a Plainfield. At the time, it was rare for women to own property. Despite this, everything that was purchased was in Augusta's name. She kept their two-story home in pristine condition. The L shaped farmhouse was white on the outside, and it possessed three porches. Those who visited the Gein family would walk into the downstairs foyer. The first door on the left led to the parlor. The parlor had fine furniture, with lace curtains. A beautiful rug and a picture of what appeared to be Augusta's mother hanging on the wall. Beyond the parlor, was Augusta and Georges bedroom. To the right of the foyer was the kitchen and dining area. The house did not have any electricity, so Augusta cooked all the family meals on a wood stove. She also had a sewing machine placed in front of one of the kitchen windows. Attached to the kitchen were the panty and shed, known as the summer kitchen. The summer kitchen was a plain wooden room with part of it having a dirt floor. This is where George would butcher their cows and pigs. The staircase in the foyer led to the bedrooms that belonged to Henry and Eddie. Everyone was expected to do their part to maintain a neat house and to do their share of work on the farm.

The Gein family farm provided most everything they needed. On occasion, they went to town to pick up the few things they didn't have. The nearest neighbors and people in town most likely noticed how distant the Gein's were. Augusta had no interest in making friends, nor did she want Henry and Eddie to play with the local children. The Gein house and farm was a substantial place compared to the humble homes in the area. People probably thought Augusta was too proud to associate with others, seeing how she would carry herself out and about. Though, Augusta did not concern herself with the opinions of people that she perceived as worldly.

In the evening, everyone would gather around in the fire lite parlor to hear Augusta preach from the bible. She felt that it was her duty to provide moral training for her two sons. She instilled in their minds that everyone is sinful, especially women. She told them to stay away from women because in her opinion, they are instruments of the devil. This had a lasting impact on her sons, especially Eddie.

Henry and Eddie attended Roche-a-Cri grade school. It was a modest one-room schoolhouse. Eddie was shy but wanted to fit in and make friends. Unfortunately, Eddie was often bullied by his peers. They made fun of his droopy eye lid and feminine mannerisms. These mannerisms were most likely developed due to his mother's dominance in his life. Eddie was shy and bashful. At times, he would randomly laugh in class, as an attempt to try to get attention. It was very hard for Eddie to relate to his peers. Sadly, boys in his class made fun of how he talked and cried easily. This deeply hurt Eddie thus causing him to believe that his mother was right about everyone being evil. Eddie was a good student, and he excelled in reading, but his parents felt that it would be best for him to stay at home and work on the farm, once he finished with the 7th grade.

Since Eddie did not have friends, he had a few hobbies that he enjoyed. In his spare time, Eddie loved reading and playing instruments. He had a harmonica, accordion and a violin. Eddie also enjoyed hunting for small game with his older brother Henry.

As Eddie and Henry grew older, they remained living at home. Eddie sometimes dreamed about being a doctor. He enjoyed studying the family medical book they had at home. He especially enjoyed the parts of the book that showed detailed drawings of human anatomy. Eddie never felt comfortable in his own skin and often wondered what it would be like to be a female. Perhaps he felt that Augusta would love him more if he was a girl.

Ch. 3

The Dairy Farm

The Gein family could not afford to modernize the family home. They remained living without electricity and indoor plumbing. Augusta came to realize despite her efforts; she could not help a man that was not willing to help himself. This caused her pity for him to turn into disgust. She could not understand why he lacked the motivation to overcome his problem, after having so many opportunities to succeed. Augusta was determined that she was going to have a successful life with or without his help. Many people have painted the picture of Augusta being a domestic tyrant. It is important to recognize the insurmountable effort that she made to hold the family together. Though it does not excuse the fact that it was wrong of Augusta to try to manipulate her sons into staying on the family farm. George was unreliable and abusive when he was drunk. Augusta was terrified of the thought of her son's getting married and leaving her to deal with George and a farm to take care of. George's health was declining rapidly. He was suffering from jaw cancer and had a leaky heart valve. On April 1, 1940, George died of heart failure. He was 66 years old. There was no outpouring of grief from the family. Augusta was just happy that she did not have to care for him anymore. By this time, World War 11 had started. Henry was too old to join, but Eddie felt that it was his duty to enlist. They rejected him due to his droopy eyelid. It slightly impaired his vision and made him unfit for the service. Augusta was relieved and they were able to continue their life on the farm.

Ch. 4

The Fire

In 1944, Henry and Eddie were burning brush on the property. Suddenly, they lost control of the fire. Eddie called for help and reported to the police that Henry was missing. However, when the police arrived, Eddie led them directly to where Henry's body was lying. Mysteriously, there were bruises on the back of Henry's head. It was clear that Henry had been dead for quite some time. After the autopsy, it was reported that Henry's death was due to asphyxiation. Henry was only 43 years old.

The news of Henry's death shocked and devastated Augusta. Suddenly, she had a stroke and was hospitalized. When she was well enough to return home, Eddie cared for her every need. Eddie was heartbroken to see his mother in such a fragile state. Augusta was very resilient, and she was determined to get well. Throughout the illness, she tried to maintain a positive attitude. Eddie was impressed that she never complained. Even though she could barely see and could hardly walk, she tried to help Eddie cook. She did not want to feel helpless, and she did not want Eddie doing all the work. Perhaps Augusta felt guilty for all the years of being so hard on Eddie. Now, she was fully dependent upon him. Augusta did not want to remain in such a vulnerable position. She was trying to learn how to walk again and wanted to surprise the doctor and nurses at the Wild Rose hospital. Fortunately, Augusta's determination paid off, and she became well again.

Eddie remembered that right before Augusta had her stroke, he had her accompany him to pick up a load of hay from a man named Mr. Smith. When they arrived, they could see that Mr. Smith owned dogs. Augusta was horrified because Mr. Smith had beaten several puppies to death and piled them up under a brush pile. Eddie believed that the combination of this event and Henry's death caused Augusta to have a stroke. Some people believe that Eddie was responsible for Henry's death. Henry was much more independent than Eddie and most likely expressed his frustration towards Augusta's controlling ways. It is also likely that he criticized Eddie for having an unhealthy attachment towards their mother. Henry wanted to settle down and have a family of his own. He purchased land across the street from the Gein farm, planning to build a house on it. Henry met a local woman and fell in love with her. She was divorced and had a child. Henry intended to marry her, but Augusta was unhappy because she did not believe in divorce. She felt that it was wrong for Henry to marry this woman. This series of events could have been the reason why Eddie hated Henry. So, the day that they were burning brush presenting Eddie the perfect opportunity to kill Henry and make it seem like it was an accident. If this was the case, it is possible that Eddie confessed his sin to Augusta. When she saw the puppies that had been beaten to death, it could have caused to her to think about what Eddie had done to Henry. Thus, causing her to become overwhelmed with emotion, to the point where she had a stroke.

Eddie was hoping to put the past behind him and focus on the joy of having his mother all to himself. Sadly, one year after recovering from her first stroke, Augusta had a second stroke that she did not

recover from. She died on December 29, 1945.
Augusta was 67 years old.

Eddie blamed himself for her death. He felt that if
he had not taken her to pick up hay, she would still
be alive. This thought continued to haunt him.
Augusta's family arrived from La crosse to attend her
funeral. They wanted to stay with Eddie, but they
quickly changed their minds once they saw the state
of his home. During the funeral, Eddie could not
contain his sorrow. He was sobbing uncontrollably.
He just lost the one person that held his world
together. Eddie was now all alone in his decaying
farmhouse. Years of being expected to keep things
neat and tidy were no longer a concern to Eddie. All
he could think about was how much he missed his
mother. She was the one in charge. Without her, he
felt lost, lonely, and hopeless. He no longer had a
desire to maintain the farm or himself. He sold the
cattle and leased out some of his farmland for
income.

During this time, Eddie began to dive more deeply
into his inner fantasies. He regularly read sexualized
detective magazines and enjoyed learning about
nazis and south sea cannibals. Eddie was amused by
gruesome tells that others would find repulsive and

disturbing. Eddie knew his mother would never approve of what he was reading but he lost the motivation to care. He was all alone and felt that he had no one to keep him accountable.

The local Plainfield residents viewed Eddie as odd but harmless. He was a mild-mannered man that was considered pleasant to have around. Eddie did not have many friends, but he regularly spent time with a local teenage boy named Bob Hill. Bob Hill's parents owned a grocery store in Plainfield. On occasion, they would invite Eddie to join them for supper. Georgia Foster lived across the street from the Hill family. Occasionally, Georgia would ask Eddie to baby sit for her. Eddie enjoyed being with the children and would often bring them candy and play games with them. Eddie also worked on threshing crews. During lunch time, the housewives would provide meals for the men on the crew. Eddie was very polite. He would always be the last one to serve himself, and the last one to take a seat at the table. After lunch, the men would gather outside to smoke and talk. Eddie would linger in the kitchen with the women. He naturally felt more comfortable in this setting and would always offer to help with the dishes. Sometimes the women would catch Eddie staring at them, it made them a little uncomfortable, but they always felt sorry for the shy and lonely bachelor.

Eddie regularly endured being picked on by the men that he worked with. Sometimes, they took their practical jokes too far. This bothered Eddie but he always tried not to show it. Many times, he would not receive payments for the jobs or favors that he would do for people. Because of this, Eddie's resentment towards people grew. He felt like everyone was wanting to take advantage of him. If someone came to visit him, it was only because they wanted something. Eddie felt used up and alone. He missed his mother and thought about how true her words were. The people of Plainfield really are sinful. The outside world is just a terrible place.

Ch. 5

The Graveyard

On occasions, Eddie suffered from hallucinations. He would see faces in the leaves and would see and hear them mocking him. Eddie could hear his mother's voice from beyond the grave, telling him to be good. He was often horrified by a smell that smelled like decaying flesh. It was as if an evil spirit was tormenting him, preying on the vulnerable state of Eddie's mind. Eddie would also experience a daze like state. Whenever he would feel it coming over him, he would pray, and the feeling would go away. Other times, it would overtake him. Eddie's inner fantasies were becoming a reality.

The local high school boys would mow the Plainfield cemetery in the summertime. They would often see Eddie visiting his mother's grave. When Eddie saw them, he would stop and say hello and would chit chat for a bit. Eddie was shy and memorized little stories and jokes to share with others. It was most likely Eddie's way of avoiding awkward conversations. When Eddie was alone in the cemetery, he would stand over his mother's grave and talk to her. His grief would overwhelm him in those moments. After his mother died, he tried to dig up her body but was unsuccessful. Sometimes coffins are buried in concrete, to prevent the grave from sinking. Eddie decided that since he could not dig up his mother, he would find someone that resembled her.

Eddie believed that he was an instrument of God possessing the power to raise the dead. Eddie would sit in his cold and junk littered farmhouse, reading the local obituaries. He was hoping to find someone that would be a good substitute for his mother. The body of a middle-aged woman was recently buried. Therefore, the soil was still soft. Eddie, wanting to be undisturbed, waited until it was dark. Grabbing his shovel, lantern, and crowbar, he headed for the cemetery. He had made many nighttime visits and this time he was not going home empty handed. Eddie began to dig as quickly as he could. He finally reached the coffin and eagerly opened the lid. Disturbing the corpse from her peaceful slumber, he scooped her up and loaded her into his vehicle. After bringing home his prize, in the dim lite room of Eddie's house he laid down the corpse. Eddie felt the rush of excitement as he studied her. He wanted to become the woman that he admired so much. Eddie taking the skin, began working away at his sewing machine, recreating the woman that he loved.

Eddie continued to rob graves from the Plainfield, Spirit Land, and Hancock cemeteries. He made things out of the body parts, being inspired by the stories that he read. Eddie peeled the face off the corpse's skull. He would preserve it to hang it on the wall like a trophy. He often applied red lipstick to the corpse's lips. He was proud of his creations and felt that he was no longer alone in his house. No one knew about the madness that was going on inside Eddie's mind.

Bob Hill and his younger brother accompanied Eddie in his home to play cards. Eddie was always good with children. He could relate to them more than he could adults. When Bob Hill and his younger brother saw the faces on Eddie's wall, Eddie simply explained that they were shrunken heads sent to him by a relative from the Philippines. Bob told his parents, and it became a running joke in town. "Odd ball Eddie has shrunken heads in his house." The children viewed Eddie's house as haunted and were always afraid to pass by it. They didn't fear Eddie, they just feared the house. It was as if they could feel the evil presence that resided there.

Georgia Foster's husband ran into to Eddie one day and began chatting with him about random things. They started talking about their homes. Since the Foster's had a growing family, they knew that they needed a bigger home. Eddie wanting a smaller home thought it might be a good idea to swap houses. The Foster's decided to pay Eddie a visit to look at his farmhouse. Georgia was shocked by how filthy and junky Eddie's house was. Though, she reminded herself that she was just there to look at the layout of the house. Eddie shut a few doors so that they could not see inside of those rooms. The Fosters were never uncomfortable with Eddie. However, when Georgia joked with Eddie about his shrunken heads, she saw a wild and angry look in his eyes. That was the only time she felt uneasy with him. Eddie realizing that she was joking, smiled and went along with the joke telling her, "They are down here in the pantry." After their short visit, they agreed that it would be a good idea to swap houses. Later, it was Eddie who decided to withdrawal from agreement.

Eddie became very uncomfortable with people being in his home. He decided that he had too much to hide and was no longer willing to open his doors to anyone. The parlor and his mother's rooms were the only rooms that were still in pristine condition. Eddie, wanting it to remain that way, boarded up those rooms as if it were a shrine for his departed mother. He mainly lived in the kitchen and in the foyer, which he fixed up to be his bedroom. Eddie laid on his bed daydreaming about a woman that he had recently met at a local tavern. She reminded him so much of his mother.

Ch.6

The Tavern

Eddie knew a woman named Adeline Watkins. She lived with her widowed mother in Plainfield. Eddie would help them on occasion, with whatever they needed. At times, Adeline felt like she was taking advantage of Eddie, because he seemed like such a sweet person, willing to do anything for her. Like Eddie, Adeline loved to read. She enjoyed discussing books with him. Most of the time, Eddie talked about the detective stories that he read. He would explain what the criminal did and what kind of mistakes he had made in trying to cover his tracks. Sometimes, Eddie and Adeline would go to town to get a milkshake or to watch a movie. Adeline felt like their relationship was blossoming. However, Eddie did not feel the same. Adeline did not always get along with her mother. Eddie was bothered by that and knew that there was no future with her, since he could not straighten her out about the matter.

Adeline liked to drink and would ask Eddie to take her to the local taverns that she enjoyed. Eddie was never comfortable with the idea of going. He was not fond of drinking beer. She felt like she had to practically drag him into a tavern. Adelines mother really like Eddie. She asked him to bring Adeline home by a certain time and Eddie, respecting that, always brought her home at that exact time. This pleased Adelines mother very much. Eddie always had a pretty good reputation amongst the people of Plainfield. Some expressed that he was a little peculiar and did not smell very well, but other than that he was known to be nice and helpful.

Eddie knew that Adeline was not the one for him and he wished that somehow, he could meet the right girl. A girl with good morals that he could admire like his mother Augusta. Eddie was always thinking about his mother and how much he missed her. Soon he was about to meet a woman that would make him feel like he was seeing his mother again.

Eddie was willing to do odd jobs to make ends meet. He drove to the town of Pine Grove, just north of Plainfield. His purpose for this was to meet a man at the Fox Head Tavern, to talk about a job. Eddie was hoping this man would hire him. When they arrived to discuss the matter, Eddie felt like a fish out of water and unlike the others he decided to order coffee from the bar owner named Mary Hogan. The locals called her Bloody Mary. People who frequented the tavern described her as being foul mouthed, tough, and jovial. When Eddie met the fifty-five-year-old Mary Hogan, he quickly recognized that she was of German descent and very much resembled his mother. This of course, caused Eddie to develop a fascination for her. When he looked at her, he saw his mother but was repulsed by Mary's worldly demeanor. Mary Hogan was known to have had a very rough past. She was from Chicago and had been married several times. She had a daughter who was put in foster care. Mary moved to the town of Pine Grove to get away from her abusive ex-husband.

When Eddie stared at her, he wondered why God allowed his mother to die. Augusta was like a saint on earth. Yet, this woman is so worldly and still living a good life. Eddie felt that this was unfair and believed in his heart that justice was in his hands.

A lot of the local men enjoyed taking a break from hunting or working to have a beer. Mary Hogan's tavern was a busy place. She lived in a small room located at the back of the tavern. Perhaps it was because of her abusive husband or her rough past, Mary Hogan was always afraid of strangers and kept the tavern doors locked during the day. She would only let people in that she knew. She kept the tavern doors open in the evening, and she had a revolver ready in a drawer in her room. Eddie knew that he needed to have Mary Hogan all alone to carry out his plan.

December was a hard month for Eddie. It was the month that he lost his beloved mother. With an overwhelming amount of emotion inside, on December 8th, 1954, Eddie decided it was the day to pay Mary Hogan a visit. Eddie, seeing that she was all alone, grabbed his 32. Mauser pistol and headed inside the tavern. Mary was sitting at a table reading and drinking a cup of coffee. When she saw Eddie enter the tavern, she recognized him. Mary felt comfortable with him, remembering how pleasant and polite he was. After making small talk Eddie walked behind her and shot her in the back of the head. She immediately fell out of her chair onto the floor. After he took a sip of her coffee, he stole all the cash that she had and quickly dragged her out of the tavern. He loaded her body into his green 1951 Dodge pickup truck and drove home.

A few hours later, a man stopped by the tavern to pick up some ice cream for his daughter. He was horrified to discover an overturned chair and a large amount of blood smeared on the floor. He immediately called for help. When the police arrived, they discovered the bullet cartridge matching a 32. caliber pistol. Mary Hogan was missing and there was hardly enough evidence to know how to move forward with the investigation. Everyone in Plainfield talked and tried to figure out what could have happened to Mary Hogan.

Elmo Ueek was a farmer and Eddie's neighbor. He recalled joking with Eddie about Mary Hogan, since Eddie was a bachelor. Elmo told Eddie, "If you had married her, she would be at the farm cooking for you instead of being missing." Eddie replied, "she's not missing. She is at the farm right now." Elmo just laughed, not thinking anything of Eddie's peculiar comment. Elmo knew Eddie was different and he always enjoyed joking with Eddie.

Georgia Foster, Irene Hill and Eddie ran into each other in a local Plainfield store. They began to discuss the disappearance of Mary Hogan. Georgia said to Irene, "I believe I know what happened to Mary Hogan. I think Eddie ran off with her because you know he is such a lady killer." Everyone laughed and Eddie replied, "Yeah and yum yum was she good." Georgia replied, "Oh my gosh Eddie what a terrible thing to say. "No one knew that Mary Hogan was really in Eddie's home.

Eddie enjoyed talking about women to the men that he worked with, but he never experienced having a physical relationship with a woman. Though, it is possible that he had sex with the dead body of Mary Hogan. It is also possible that he cooked parts of her body and ate them. Since Eddie wanted victims that reminded him of his mother, it is very likely that he could have been sexually attracted to his mother. Augusta was Eddie's entire world. Since she tried to keep him away from women, he wanted her to fulfill every need and every desire that he had.

Eddie learned a lot from his parents. His mother taught him how to sew, and his father taught him how to butcher an animal and how to tan the hide. He put his skills to use with the corpses that he collected. However, nothing excited him as much as having a fresh victim. One that he had killed himself, as a sacrifice to be reborn into his mother. Eddie was now able to begin working on his masterpiece. He made leggings from skin, preserved the upper torso of a woman. He peeled off the face, having the hair still attached to wear as a mask. Once the skin suit was complete, he put on the leggings and the torso. He placed a woman's preserved genitalia on top of his own. Lastly, he put on the face mask and capered around his house and yard. Remembering how even as a child, he always wished to be a girl. His fantasy had finally come true. He had transformed himself into the woman he always dreamed of becoming. He no longer had to hate himself. Covering his body with this skin suit was covering all the years of pain, insecurity, and rage. He now could feel like his mother, who possessed all the confidence that he had always lacked. No matter how hard life could be, he now had the ability to escape from it all.

Ch. 7

The Hardware Store

Bernice Worden owned the Worden Hardware store in Plainfield. Everyone in the community knew and respected Bernice. She received the honor of being the first female citizen of the week in July of 1956.

Eddie was one of her frequent customers. He began to develop a fascination for Bernice. She was a strong, independent, middle-aged woman. She reminded him of his beloved mother. Whenever he went to the hardware store, he would ask Bernice if she wanted to go roller skating with him. Bernice was clearly not interested and probably felt some dread every time she saw the lonely bachelor enter her store. Despite this, she remained helpful and friendly to Eddie.

By this time, Eddie was fifty-one years old. It was the month of November, and almost all the men in Plainfield were hunting for deer. Eddie had no interest in deer hunting. He claimed that the sight of blood made him feel sick. Eddie went to the hardware store on Friday, to check on the price of anti-freeze. Bernice's son Frank was in the hardware store at the time. Eddie asked Frank if he would be deer hunting in the morning. Frank replied that he might, and Eddie happily knew that Bernice would most likely be all alone in the store.

Plainfield was like a ghost town on Saturday during hunting season. Eddie went home and went to bed that night, knowing he had a big day ahead of him. Eddie woke up that Saturday morning on November 16, 1957. After he got dressed and ate his favorite cereal with warm milk, he stepped outside feeling the cold Wisconsin air on his face. It had been raining earlier that morning and it reminded Eddie of his mother. She would always call him inside when it rained to pray over him. She would say, "God has sent this storm as he sent it to Noah, to wash away the sins of woman. Woman is evil." Eddie was overcome with emotion. It had finally stopped raining and Eddie walked to his car, ready to pay Bernice Worden a visit.

He drove his maroon 1949 sedan to the hardware store. After arriving, he asked Bernice if he could buy some antifreeze. She filled the jug for Eddie, took his money, and wrote up a sales receipt. After Eddie put the antifreeze in his car, He decided to go back into the store, to tell Bernice that he was interested in trading in his Marlin rifle for another rifle. He explained that his rifle only fired .22 short and that he wanted a rifle that could fire short, long, and long rifle. Bernice was happy to help and took down one of the rifles that she felt would suit him. As he began to look it over, Bernice turned her back to Eddie to look out the window. As she was making small talk, Eddie reached into his pocket and took out a .22 bullet and immediately loaded the rifle.

Eddie remembered one of the old men in the community, telling him a story about Bernice Worden. He told Eddie that many years ago, Mr. Worden was dating the daughter of a dentist. This young girl was in love with Mr. Worden. The young girl became heartbroken because Mr. Worden left her to be with Bernice and he eventually married Bernice. Sadly, the young girl committed suicide because she could not get over Mr. Worden. The old man also told Eddie that years later, Bernice had an affair with a married man in town. Eddie believed these stories and viewed Bernice as a wicked woman that deserved punishment for the pain that she caused.

Eddie raised his rifle and shot Bernice in the back of her head. Eddie then dragged her out of the store and loaded her body into the store's truck. Eddie drove the Hardware store truck to a remote pine forest. Eddie then walked back to the hardware store and drove his vehicle to the pine forest. Eddie took Bernice's body out of the truck and loaded it into his car. Bernard Muschinski owned the gas station across the street from the hardware store. When he saw someone driving the hardware store truck. He wasn't alarmed because figured it was a man that Bernice had hired to run deliveries. Anyone who passed by the store, did not find it to be unusual that the store was closed. Especially, since most everyone was in the woods hunting.

Elmo Ueek was fortunate to kill a deer that day. However, it was unfortunate that it happened to fall on Eddie's land. Elmo knew how Eddie felt about people trespassing on his land, and Elmo certainly didn't want to get caught. By this time, Eddie was heading back to his farmhouse. Eddie could see other men passing by with their kill of the day. However, Eddie was especially proud of his own.

Elmo felt like he was caught red handed when he saw Eddie drive by. Elmo was embarrassed but was also surprised by how fast Eddie was driving. Elmo knew his guilt would eat him up inside if he did not apologize and explain to Eddie what had happened. That afternoon, Elmo paid Eddie a visit. Eddie was outside next to his car, removing the snow chains from the tires. Elmo thought that was a very strange thing to do, especially in November. Elmo knowing Eddie was odd, decided to overlook it and proceeded with his apology. Eddie didn't seem to care; he was completely occupied by the task at hand. Elmo realizing this, decided to leave Eddie alone.

A little while later, Bob Hill and his sister showed up at Eddie's house. He asked Eddie if he could get some help installing a car battery. Eddie had blood all over his hands. Eddie said, "Let me clean up and then I will be glad to help you." Bob and his sister did not think anything of the blood, since it was deer season. Eddie helped them install the battery and afterwards, they invited him to stay for supper. Eddie always looked forward to a good home cooked meal, since he was used to eating simple things like canned pork and beans at his home.

Eddie had no idea that Frank Worden had discovered that his mother was missing. Frank did not understand why the store was locked, with the lights still on, and why the store's truck was missing. He entered the hardware store and noticed a trail of smeared blood on the floor. He realized that the trail of blood led to the back door and out to where the truck usually sat. Frank was so distraught and was determined to find her. Frank Worden was the Deputy Sheriff and he called Arthur Schley, who was the sheriff. Sheriff Schley had only been a sheriff for a little over a month. Frank saw that the cash register was missing, and he saw a sales receipt with Eddie's name on it. He knew that Eddie had been bothering his mother lately and he also knew that Eddie was the last person to see her. Frank was boiling over with anger and knew they had to find Eddie. The officers arrived at Eddie's house and realized that he was not home. They viewed this as their opportunity to search Eddies house.

Ch.8

The Hill's Home

Eddie felt comfortable with the Hill family. He appreciated them allowing him to stay for supper. While everyone was eating, Lester and Irene's son-in-law came in after deer hunting. He told everyone about how he saw police cars at the Worden Hardware store. He was eager to know what had happened. The family expressed their concerns while Eddie sat there quietly. No one ever suspected that the shy and lonely bachelor sitting at their table was the one who committed this terrible crime. Eddie was confident that he would not get caught, since they never figured out what had happened to Mary Hogan.

Bob wanted a ride into town to witness all the action. He asked Eddie if he would drive him. Eddie obliged and they went outside to warm up Eddie's car. By this time, officers Dan Chase and Deputy Poke Spees stopped by Hill's house to see if Eddie was there. They knew he was known to be a frequent visitor. Irene directed them outside where Eddie was warming up his car. The officer asked Eddie to roll down the window. He told Eddie that he wanted to talk with him. Eddie's heart began to race, and he was led to the squad car to be questioned. The officer began to question Eddie about his day, and he wanted all the details from beginning to end. Eddie struggled to explain the events of his day. When the officer questioned him further, Eddie said "Somebody framed me." The officer decided to play dumb and said, "framed you for what?" Eddie said, "Mrs. Worden." The officer said, "What about Mrs. Worden." Eddie said, "Well she's dead, isn't she?" It was then, that the officer knew he had the right man. Everyone in town knew that Mrs. Worden was missing but no one knew that she had been killed. They arrested Eddie and were eager to interrogate him.

Back at Eddie's farmhouse, officers were prepared to enter Eddie's home. It was a creepy old house, very dark and gloomy. They were not prepared for the horrific discoveries that they were about to make. Sheriff Schley and Captain Schoephoerster realized that all the doors were locked and there were old raggedy shades and curtains over the windows. However, they realized that the shed door was open. The shed was attached to the kitchen. Without a search warrant, and with their flashlights, they began their illegal search through the dark and junky shed. Meanwhile, Schley bumped into something hanging in the shed. He turned to shine his flashlight on it. To his incredible horror, it was Bernice Worden. Schley said, "my gosh there she is!" Bernice Worden's body was hanging upside down by her heels. Her head was decapitated, and her body had been gutted like a deer. Schley stumbled out of the shed and began vomiting onto the snow. Schoephoerster came running out behind him and radioed for help. They could only imagine what other terrible things awaited them in Eddie's house of horrors.

The officers cautiously made their way inside the rest of the dark house. They found strange items such as a collection of used chewing gum and old dentures. The smell in the house was intolerable, and they began to discover Eddie's gruesome handiwork. The officers found bowls made from human skulls and utensils made from human bones, they couldn't believe their eyes and wondered if Eddie was a cannibal. They discovered chairs and a lampshade upholstered from human skin, handbags and gloves upholstered and fashioned from human skin. After seeing the amount of body parts, they began to think that Eddie was a serial killer. They found a shade pull made from human lips, a waste bucket made from human skin, four noses, and a belt made from human nipples. They found fingernails and a box full of nine female genitals. Eddie had sprinkled them with salt. He painted one of them silver and had a red ribbon tied around it. They also found a young girls dress and two female genitals, that appeared to be from a teenager around the age of fourteen. Once they discovered Eddie's skin suit, they were shocked and tried to understand what would drive a man to such madness. They knew Eddie was proud of his grizzly creations. Eddie had skulls mounted on his bed posts and had women's faces mounted on the wall like they were his trophies. One officer found a paper bag with hair sticking out of it. He grabbed a hold of the hair and when he pulled it out, he realized it was someone that he recognized. It was the face of Mary Hogan. The mystery had finally been solved. They also found a burlap sack that had steam rising from it. They were certain that it was another body part. They retrieved what was inside and saw that it was Bernice Worden's head. Eddie had attached strings to it with intensions of hanging it on the wall. The officers could not determine how many victims there were, due to the amount of body parts that were found.

All these discoveries were made within a few rooms. Officers noticed that some of the rooms had been boarded up. They could only imagine what awful things could be waiting behind the walls of these rooms. They immediately began tearing down the boards covering the doors, only to find dusty rooms that were kept in perfect order. They realized that these were the rooms belonging to Eddie's mother. One room was the parlor, and the room next to it was her bedroom. Everything remained the way that Augusta had left it. In her bedroom, there was a bible on her nightstand beside of her bed. Resting on a lace covered dresser, was a hairbrush. It still had her long white hair stuck in the bristles. The room was very musty and dusty. It was obvious that nothing had been disturbed in years. It was once a very nice farmhouse. Sadly, Eddie turned it into a house of death. All the terrible findings had to be hauled away as evidence. News reporters stormed the property and soon the world would know the name of Ed Gein.

Meanwhile, Eddie was locked in a jailhouse in the city of Wautoma. Everyone was eager to understand what caused Eddie to commit these horrible atrocities.

Ch.9

The Jailhouse

Eddie was kept in a cell, located in the rear of the jailhouse. Sheriff Schley and his family lived in the front of the building. Schley was traumatized by what he had seen and was eager to know if Eddie had confessed or not. Eddie was unwilling to talk to investigators. Schley was so upset by this that he tried to force Eddie to talk by slamming him up against the wall. This caused Eddie to become more withdrawn, and everyone's frustrations became more intense. While the investigators were interrogating Eddie, they tried to make him as comfortable as possible. They offered him plenty to eat and drink. They treated him like a guest that they wanted to impress. This helped Eddie feel more relaxed. Once they confronted Eddie with all the evidence that they had, he began to confess to the murders of Bernice Worden and Mary Hogan.

Naturally, everyone wanted to pin all the unsolved murders in the area on Eddie. When he was asked about the disappearance of eight-year-old Georgia Jean Weckler and missing teenager Evelyn Hartley, Eddie denied being involved with their disappearance. Eddie was also confronted with the disappearance of two hunters. Victor Travis and Ray Burgess. They were two hunters that had recently disappeared in Plainfield. They were last seen at a local bar flashing a large amount of cash. They left the bar to go hunting and disappeared. The two men left behind a jacket and their dog in the woods near Eddie's property. People like Elmo Ueek knew how Eddie hated poachers. It is possible that Eddie had something to do with their disappearance, even though he denied that as well.

During this time, the residents of Plainfield were overwhelmed by the amount of publicity their village was receiving. Traffic was bumper to bumper, and they were constantly bombarded by reporters, asking questions about their neighbor Eddie. One neighbor remembered a foul smell coming from Eddie's property. He was deeply disturbed to learn that it was because Eddie would burn the body parts that he did not have any use for. The more information that came out in the newspapers about what Eddie had done, the more shocked and horrified the people of Plainfield were. They could not believe that this had been going on in their community all along.

Everyone had their doubts about Eddie being a grave robber. The only way to know if he really dug up the corpses would be to exhume one of the graves that he claimed to have desecrated. With some dread knowing it was a sensitive issue for the families, they headed for the Plainfield cemetery. It was on November 25, 1957, that they exhumed the caskets of Eleanor Adams and Mabel Everson. They found that the casket of Eleanor Adams had nothing in it besides a crowbar. Mabel Everson's casket was empty, and they found a pile of bones, dentures, clothing, and a wedding ring in the soil. These findings confirmed that Eddie was telling the truth.

While Eddie was in the Wautoma jailhouse, he was thinking about how his mother would be so ashamed of what he had done. Augusta being very religious, taught Eddie about the bible and the importance of living a righteous life. Though it is clear, that Augusta's views on being a follower of God, were a bit strange. She was hindered by her strict and legalistic upbringing. Thus, causing

Augusta to most likely not know the sweetness of having a personal relationship with a loving God. A God who forgives us and encourages us to live a life devoted to Him and does not condemn us when we fail. We are all sinners, and we desperately need our Creator. God loves us so much that He sent his only son to die for us. In doing this, He wiped away our sins so that we can spend eternity with Him. All we must do is believe in Him, know that He is God and decide to devote our lives to Him. God created us and He has a desire to show us His amazing purpose for our lives. He expects progress from us not perfection. God had a great plan for Eddie's life. Unfortunately, Eddie allowed things to get in the way of that plan. Eddie committed horrible sins, but God can forgive those sins. If Eddie asked God to forgive him and believed that God is his Lord and Savior, then Eddie would go to heaven. In Luke chapter 23, the criminal on the cross next to Jesus, asked to be forgiven and believed. The criminal said to Jesus, "Jesus remember me when you come into your kingdom." Jesus said to him, "I tell you the truth. Today you will be with me in paradise." The criminal died knowing that he would be with his Savior in paradise forever.

Bernice Worden's funeral was held at the Plainfield United Methodist Church. She was in an open casket. It was very important for her body to be put back together and to be buried with dignity.

Thirty-three-year-old Reverand Kenneth Engleman of the Wautoma methodist church, felt in his heart that God wanted him to see Eddie. He wanted to spiritually encourage him. When Reverend Engleman arrived at the Wautoma Jailhouse, he was met by a large group of reporters. The reporters were frustrated because they were not allowed to interview Eddie. However, the Reverand was allowed to speak with Eddie. When the Reverand approached Eddie, he said "Mr. Gein I am here to give you spiritual help. I know that this has been a hard day for you." Eddie was immediately touched by his words and the Reverand spoke with Eddie about his crimes and about the death of his parents. He could clearly see that Eddie was broken and remorseful for the things that he had done. Eddie described in tears how sorry he was for the pain that he had caused others. Eddie also expressed that after his parents died, it had left him feeling very empty. Eddie was comforted and encouraged by the Reverand. They knelt in front of the prison bed and prayed together.

Eddie wept convulsively. After the prayer, The Reverand left Eddie with a book of scriptures. This really encouraged Eddie. After the visit, Eddie told Sheriff Schley that he hoped the Reverand would visit him again. The Reverand already had plans to visit Eddie again the following Thursday. The reporters were very jealous of Reverand Engleman, because they were not allowed to conduct any interviews with Eddie.

Since Eddie had confessed to the murder of Mary Hogan and Bernice Worden, it was time for Eddie to stand before a judge. Eddie was charged with murder and pleaded not guilty for reason of insanity. In result, Eddie did not go to prison, and he was escorted to Central State Hospital in Wisconsin for the criminally insane. The Plainfield residents were outraged. They knew that Eddie would have a good life at the mental hospital and felt that it was not the appropriate punishment for what he had done. Many people in Plainfield wanted to take matters into their own hands and give Eddie what they felt he deserved.

Several people reported that they were given venison as gift from Eddie. After realizing that he was not a deer hunter, and after finding out about the horrible crimes that he committed, they instantly became sick. They believed that they had eaten some of Eddie's victims. Perhaps, Eddie did this out of revenge, because of how he was treated.

While Eddie was at Central State Hospital, he went through many tests. Doctors determined that he was suffering from schizophrenia. Eddie seemed to be in good health, and he had a relatively normal IQ. However, he did complain about having frequent headaches and stomach pains. He also complained about hallucinating. Eddie was happy about being at the hospital. He was thankful to be well cared for and to live in a nice clean place. Eddie did make a suspicious comment to police investigators when they were discussing Eddies visit with the doctors that examined him. Eddie said, "I think I have them pretty well convinced." Could it be that Eddie was a cunning manipulator just like Augusta? Perhaps Eddie tried to convince the doctors that he was insane, to avoid going to prison.

Eddie remained at the hospital until his insanity hearing on November 21, 1957. At the hearing, Eddie was deemed mentally incompetent to stand trial and was recommitted to Central State Hospital. Meanwhile, many curious people from all over came to visit Plainfield. An auction was held at Eddie's

home and around two thousand people showed up.
Eddie's possessions were sold to pay for the lawsuits
filed by the relatives of Eddie's victims. Many
Plainfield residents were concerned that someone
would buy Eddie's house and turn it into a museum.
Not surprisingly, the house burned down and though
it was not proven, arson was suspected.
Interestingly, the fire chief was Frank Worden. When
Eddie found out his house burned down, he simply
said "Just as well." Everyone wanted to put the past
behind them, including Eddie.

Ch. 10

The Hospital

Eddie's life greatly improved at Central State Hospital. He was well-behaved, spent lots of time reading and doing jobs that were available for the patients. The hospital staff noticed that he did not interact much with other patients and that Eddie seemed to daydream a lot. Eddie remained the polite quite man that he always seemed to be. As years passed, Eddie became bored and felt that he was ready to be set free. He dreamed about moving to Australia. In 1968, he requested to be released back into society, a request that was later denied. In 1974, Eddie tried again and filed a petition to be set free, but this request was also denied. No one believed that Eddie was no longer capable of committing more terrible crimes.

Eddie was later moved to Mendota Mental Health institute in Wisconsin, where he died of lung cancer on July 26, 1984. He was seventy-seven years old.

Investigators claimed to have smelled embalming fluid when they first entered Eddie's home. This was a claim later denied by Eddie. However, it is obvious that he exposed himself to it. Embalming fluid contains formaldehyde. Formaldehyde is a chemical that is very harmful and can cause lung cancer. Eddie's home was built in the 1800's. It could have contained asbestos, since asbestos mining and manufacturing was flourishing during that time. Asbestos has a resistance to heat, water, and chemicals, thus making it an excellent insulator for ovens, boilers, and steam engines. Asbestos was often used in building materials and paint. Therefore, it is highly possible that Eddie was exposed to this, which can lead to mesothelioma and lung cancer. Eddie's home could have exposed him to lead paint as well. Lead paint was commonly used before the 1970's. Lead paint exposure can cause brain damage. It is certainly not healthy living in an environment such as this. Eddie often breathed in wood smoke from his wood stove. This would have been bad for Eddie's lungs as well as mold, which is very likely to have been an issue in Eddie's home. All these things including how junky and dusty Eddies home was, could have contributed to Eddie suffering from headaches and stomach pains, and of course him developing lung cancer later in his life.

Eddie always dreamed of being with his mother again. In death, he achieved this dream and was buried next to her in the Plainfield cemetery. Sheriff Arthur Schley died of a heart attack at the age of only forty-three. Many believe that Eddie was responsible for Schley's death due to the amount of stress that he caused Schley.

Eddie was unaware of the damage his beloved mother had afflicted upon him. Obviously, Augusta had her best interest in mind instead of her sons. It is true that Eddie loved and admired his mother. Though, it is possible that a part of him hated her as well. She controlled him to the point where he was not free to be himself and to pursue the life that he was meant to live. Some people believe that this could be the reason why he was violent towards his victims. Butchering their bodies was his way of expressing his anger and resentment towards his mother. Eddie being abused, lacking confidence, and having no direction other than living on the farm with Augusta, was setup for failure after she died.

It is easy to criticize Eddie for the things that he did but at the same time, many people feel sorry for him because they feel that he never had a chance to develop into a healthy adult. However, his difficult upbringing does not excuse the terrible things that he did. Eddie understood right from wrong.

No one can deny the fact that there is evil in this world. We see it every day and it was evident in Eddies life. Evil only has power when we give into the temptation of it. Jesus has shown us through the life that He lived, that we can defeat evil. 1 John 3:8 says "For this purpose the Son of God was manifested, that He might destroy the works of the devil. Everyone can overcome their sin. Romans 12:2 says "Do not be conformed to this world, but be transformed by the renewing of your mind, so that you may prove what the will of God is, that which is good and acceptable and perfect. Romans 12:21 also says "Do not be overcome by evil but overcome evil with good." Eddie certainly had the ability to overcome the evil that was tormenting him. Sadly, he chose to give into it. This decision not only destroyed his life but also devasted the lives around him.

Virginia Monroe
BENEATH THE SURFACE

"The thief comes only to steal, kill, and destroy. I came that they may have life and have it more abundantly."

John 10:10

Plainfield

Cemetery

Ed Gein is buried between his mother and brother.
His gravestone had been stolen. Fortunately, it has
been recovered, and It is now kept in a secret place.

This is the location where the body parts of Ed Gein's victims were buried.

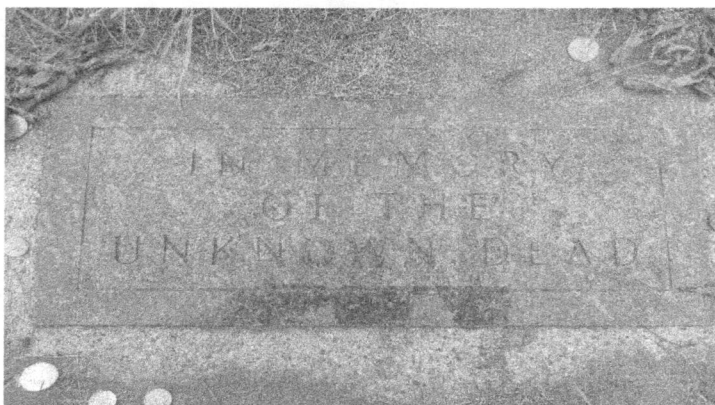

These are the victims that Ed Gein dug up.

Hancock

Cemetery

Lola Foster was one of the victims that Ed Gein dug up.

Spritland

Cemetery

These are the victims that Ed Gein dug up.

Wautoma

Union

Cemetery

Ed Gein's Property.

The location where Mary Hogan's tavern once stood.

Bernice Worden's hardware store.

The jailhouse where Ed Gein was held.

Virginia Monroe
BENEATH THE SURFACE

Author's Note

I would like to thank you for purchasing this book. I want you to know that I love and care about you. All of us are not promised tomorrow. The question that you must ask yourself is, do you know where you will go when you die? God loves you more than you can ever imagine. He wants to have a personal relationship with you. The following steps will guide you, if you would like to pursue a relationship with Him.

Recognize your need for God:

Admit you have fallen short (sinned) and need God's help and forgiveness.

Believe in Jesus:

Trust that Jesus is the son of God, who died for your sins and rose again.

Accept salvation:

Ask God for forgiveness and accept His gift of salvation through Jesus. This is done through prayer, saying something like, "I'm a sinner: I believe Jesus died for me; please save me.

Repent:

Turn away from your old way of life and commit to following God's way.

Pray daily:

Talk to God regularly, asking for guidance and strength.

Read scripture:

Make daily Bible reading a habit for direction and encouragement.

Connect with a church:

Join a local, Bible-believing church for community, worship, and teaching.

Be baptized:

This is a public declaration of your new faith in Jesus.

Live like Jesus:

Strive to be kind, honest, loving, forgiving, and patient in your daily life.

Serve others:

Follow Jesus' example by serving those in need.

Share your faith:

Let your life and words reflect Jesus to others.

Key takeaway:

This is a lifelong process of learning and growing closer to Him. We will never be perfect in this life. We will continue to sin. However, do not let this discourage you in your walk with God. God loves you no matter what. He does not condemn you; He encourages you to overcome your sins, because He wants the very best for you. With God's help, you can fulfill the purpose that He has for you and become everything He created you to be.

References

Wikipedia...

History of Wisconsin

History of La Crosse

History of Plainfield

Ed Gein the real psycho house by Kent Stolt

Books...

Deviant by Harold Schechter

Did You Hear What Eddie Gein Done? by Harold Schechter and Eric Powell

The Ed Gein Files by John Borowski

Documentaries...

Ed Gein The World's Most Evil Killers - Real Crime

Serial Killer Ed Gein the Real Leatherface - Serial Killers Worldwide

*Murderous Minds the Real Chainsaw Massacre –
Top5s*

Newspapers...

*Headlines from the Ed Gein murders – Stevens Point
Daily Journals*

Virginia Monroe
BENEATH THE SURFACE

Virginia Monroe
BENEATH THE SURFACE

Virginia Monroe
BENEATH THE SURFACE

www.ingramcontent.com/pod-product-compliance
Lightning Source LLC
Chambersburg PA
CBHW070028030426
42335CB00017B/2331